TOKYO POETRY JOURNAL

TOKYO CITY / SLICE

VOLUME 11 • SUMMER 2022

Copyright © 2022 Tokyo Poetry Journal

All rights remain with authors, translators, artists, etc.

Subscriptions available via our website (credit card, Paypal, bank transfer, or international postal money order sent to address below).

¥1500/issue or ¥2500/year for individuals
¥2500/issue or ¥3500/year for institutions.
Bank transfers to: Japan Post Bank
(Account Name: Johnson Jeffrey Richard, Bank Code 10020, Branch# 008, Account# 24951451).

ISBN 978-1-957704-03-6

Submissions are accepted on an ongoing basis. Go to topojo. com for more information.

Send postal submissions & subscription payments to:
Tokyo Poetry Journal c/o Jordan Smith
Akabori Mansion 101, Yokoteramachi 10-1
Shinjuku-ku, Tokyo 162-0831 Japan

www.topojo.com
facebook.com/tokyopoetryjournal
soundcloud.com/youtube-topojo
Instagram: @tokyopoetry
Twitter: @poetrytokyo

CONTENTS

EDITORS' LETTER

Stand behind the yellow line.

黄色線までおさがりください。

∘ ∘ ∘ ∘ ∘ ∘ ∘ ∘ ∘ ∘ ∘ ∘

Tokyo lines up when it must, but after the last train has departed, poets walk the rails and squeeze through the trap doors under the platforms. We untangle power lines hanging over like mysterious myriad-stroke kanji. Between the city slices we let some poetry bleed out.

This volume of poetry distills TOkyo TOday/TOmorrow, what the city hints at, what morse code shoes are tapping on the vacuumed train station stairs, what is lost in bilingual conversation and between one too many konbini chuhais. Taylor Mignon and Zoria Petkoska's collaborative poem "Collapsing Chuhai" encapsulates some of this *ToToTo-scape*.

This volume was a long time coming. From Drunk Poets See God in Gari Gari, when said poets would wander into Shibuya walking after midnight. From poetry collaborations taking root in Yoyogi Park. From gatherings to write poems to the full moon, shrouded in clouds. From burning poems only to recreate them with fiery inspiration. Everything you find in this city is a trigger.

"You find yourself wishing you were a perfectly folded cardboard box in Shibuya."

This is how ToPoJo editor Mat Chiappe starts his work "Matches". The neat order of garbage is a window to what life feels like in the metropolis.

Neon excitement, sculpturesque architecture, and maximalist city clutter is how ToPoJo Volume 11 cover artist Simon Kalajdjiev inhabits glitched Tokyo. Then, a fish behind a tower behind a train behind a giant robot, in the surreal art of Erica Ward. And the monochrome and fluorochrome collisions (collusions?) of artist Apolo Cacho created in Tokyo. There is always everything going on in this city.

"Shitsurei shimasu," says a voice while pushing you from behind.

An army of salarymen are exhaled out of a train only to be inhaled by the station's hallways. You are among them. You have to go to work or to the Immigration Office or you are simply there, after some random interdimensional trip. The crowd pushes you forward and you seem to lose agency.

"But I am a poet!" you want to shout, to howl. You feel sliced, like everything in Tokyo. The columns, the windows, the tiles, all lonely jigsaw puzzles of the city. You end up recollecting a couple of fragments among the bodies (*"Commodity lotteries, no night skies / banks that stilt by on the sidewalks!"* cries Andrew Hanson; *"They pulse and flicker, wheel into existence / It isn't clear what survives the rippling lights, gives rise to name and form"* recounts Kathleen Hellen; *"Buck rolls & bucks flow, dragon digests, splurge of words regurge"* chant Matthew Zuckerman and Taylor Mignon), a few slices of the city that sound literary enough to you.

Deadstreaming© trains

(*click here to buy rights to this word*)

This quote is from one of the cyber(punk) poems included in this volume by ToPoJo editor Zoria Petkoska, where she imagines a late-stage capitalist world in which every drop of creativity is for sale. The poem ends with a QR code that leads you to a website where you can buy the ending of the poem. (*We are all waiting for the birth of PoetryCoin*)

And you… you already start thinking about the price tag for the images you caught in Shinagawa. [ENTER THE CITY'S SEAL OF APPROVAL HERE]

木木林森林木木水 。 。 。井の頭公園吉祥寺 。 。 。水木木林森林木木

This volume was put together on the go. Restless Tokyo kami would be proud.

Editorial catch-ups while running to catch the last Inokashira line train. Zoom meetings and zooming past deadlines, exhausted. Fries and falafel on the park bench, balancing a laptop full of poems on one knee. The phone is a sacrifice, it falls on the stones and shatters. The laptop is safe. ToPoJo Volume 11 is safe. Pray to the technogods to send the verification code.

Tokyo has nature slices too, tucked between the concrete and the asphalt. And some of us sing to them, like Sarah Caulfield does in her poem "Akishima-shi": "*The nightsong of the vending machines' humming under the cicadas. The air smells like the memory of sun*". Like Simon Scott's night that is black and treacly: "*The night the moon opened / and all her petals / slowly / fell to earth / And from then forth / The sky was always a black black flower*". Like Jordan Smith's multilingual tangle: "故郷に帰る・市役所「で」入る・古い池に・艶っぽい蛙・新たな旗を・水の音に捧げる".

If only there were more moments like this. You hate this city for not giving you time, for not letting you enjoy, for tearing off the poet in you. But maybe that will end too. "*I'm foreign, a phase that will soon pass, as birds resettle in outstretched branches — complaining*", writes Carl Walsh.

WASEDA UNIVERSITY, 6 PM.

Only two days ago, right here, next to Murakami's new mausoleum-style library, the poet, mystic, and astral traveler Yoshimasu Gōzō almost fainted in one of his famous artistic rituals. Poetry prevails. Only one day ago, right here, ToPoJo editor Jordan Smith and Ito Hiromi commanded a poetry workshop with the stellar presence of rap music and Google Translate deformations of Mori Ogai's literature. Poetry prevails. Hours ago, right here, Master's student Kana Hozoji wrote, just before the closing of our deadline, *"Those stories, read, by, bodies, pre, mature, bodies, taught me how to identify with the collective"*. Poetry prevails. Seconds ago, right here, the sunrays sliced the clouds and the stars punctured the city and ToPoJo's Associate Editors made the final cuts on Volume 11's manuscript. Poetry unveils.

— Zoria Petkoska K. & Mat Chiappe

MAT CHIAPPE

Matches

You find yourself wishing you were a perfectly folded cardboard box in Shibuya.

You see yourself in a Ginza restaurant having visions in the glass behind that guy.

You accompany yourself into a coven of shy and noisy salarymen in Kanda, thinking, "What language is this?"

You follow yourself through Koenji, wanting to take home that amazing cowboy hat, but not everything under it, also doubting, "Should I praise that style?"

You witness yourself counting cigarette butts inside a jar on a balcony in Omotesando, not finding the words for "you so look different than in your profile."

You listen to yourself articulate the product details of a lotus-shaped plastic vagina in Nakano Central Park, persuading your ego, "This could work out."

You turn yourself contentless in a game center in Ikebukuro, laughing, not believing, yet chipping in, "I need to go," just minutes past.

You congratulate yourself for picking up that broken tape-recorder in the streets of Waseda, both it and yourself too proud to hint at the songs you liked, the same day in which you asked in your teacherlyest of voices, "Wanna come to my house?"

You catch one last scent of yourself in the most clichéd of places (Haneda airport, a *shinkansen* platform), trying not to look desperate as that couple says "so happy we met in this big town."

You blame yourself for being stood up at that temple in Asakusa, every reflection in every vending machine shouting that someone is enjoying this city more than you are.

You lose yourself in a rave of lonely cenobites in Roppongi, another night of dancing and "I missed the last train" and that everlasting idea that you are still twenty.

You sketch a wanted poster of yourself in a bar in Shinjuku, wishing you could tell this person in front of you the truth about a crime you never committed, instead just snapping back, "should we do another round?"

You pull yourself together at a gyoza home-party in Nippori, convinced that you can bear the constant vigilance of this capital, of this overly attached citybabe, so horny and immortal; "I think I love you," you spill out, resigned, as a tribute to urbanism.

You found yourself here and there in Tokyo.

But you found only yourself in Tokyo.

ALVIN WONG
Nocturnal Past-times

the tire marks of yesterday
shroud in the apparitions of footsteps
the rising office towers
those who do not leave a trace
on blasted concrete, without shadows
a sunless afternoon, aquarium panes
the sky can only grasp sparse clouds
their circuits from office to house
box lunches and the overhead train
powering the electric city
a haze of chemical lights, bodies pass
others, leaving ashen shreds in the road
cars leave a metallic dash before enveloped
in the tearing of glossy magazine advertisements
to imagine the city disappearing into a void
a runway of miniature suns, orange spokes
alter the grey highways, the neon panes
grey in the daytime now radiate in colour
orange shreds in the night, it's autumn now
and we lose old smiles in our fevered nights

Absences

Like little suns you could clasp in your hand
You would finally be able to stand for something profound
And if you accelerate

The only thing falling is you
Tilting up and down
The rear wheel powers out
The static on the television swallowed

Red houses dissolve to white
The only thing you salvage
On a summer's day, is when someone turns the volume up

By the bore of a heatwave
By the synaptic break
Outside, the raindrops fall
A little dome forms
To withstand homes and thin metal sheets
Outside, a few images,
Of stripes and echoing stars

Rolling Breaks, Walk on Night

afternoon light chiseled into ruins
charting the route of our past sunbeams
exhausting the night of its splendour
throbbing of the festivals that heightened our step
could your world have spun off the sole
clutching all of todays that lingered our doings
silver marbles ricochet off studded cabinets
were each of us to be that mountain vista
that played with the sun and moon across summer
azures maintained off electronics, restless among wavelengths
upon highways that orbited our future selves off panes
sparkling in films in beautiful sequence
open throttle, grasping the carousel
thinking to see each other again
even on painted horses or fantastic palaces
imminent in the sudden morning
where we land from our frenzies
rippling into canyons, the places we fell

ERICA WARD

Erica Ward's assemblages of urban visual metaphors function as charms and spells that capture the essence of Tokyo. Trains and power lines weave through people and robots alike, apartment blocks grow on pine bonsai, kimono-clad women play on the strings of the Tokyo Metro map.

The surreal Tokyo in Erica Ward's artwork is a dreamworld that feels simultaneously real and unreal. In the city where every street corner holds surprises and gateways to new worlds, anything seems possible.

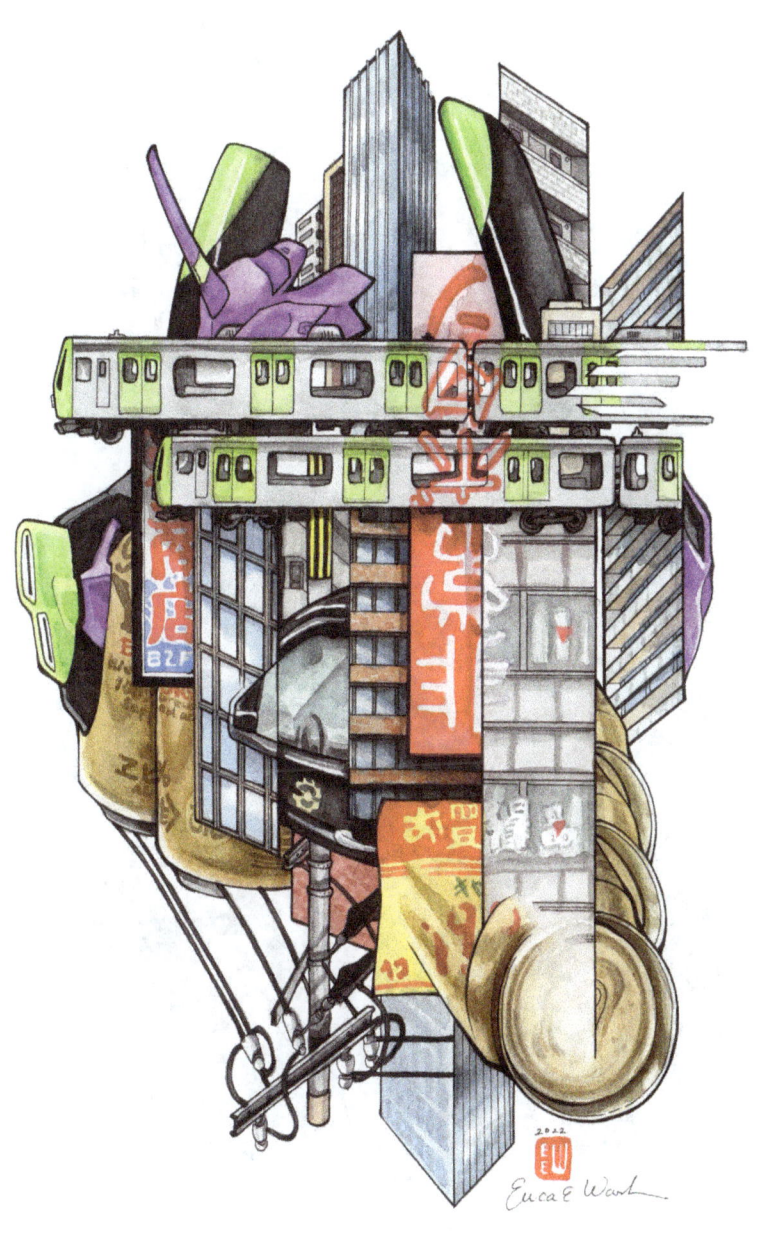

「非常ボタン」
"Hijō Botan"

「掴めない感情」
"Ungraspable Emotion"

「ケシ」
"Poppy"

ZORIA PETKOSKA K. & TAYLOR MIGNON

Collapsing Chuhai

Train-strained to a speck, breathe in........ breathe out.......
Coughing fit fast forward to fist fight, ah, masks off
Gloves on. A spitting image of a broken mirror
Dukes down — each sputum a universe— chuhai kanpai
achoo-hai, kanpai ippai, cheers to the cheerful, and then — silence
....yes
No, silence not found.
SILENCE is sold in slices here, a rare commodity,
a foie gras of force-feeding me loneliness

Step up & git yr fresh slices of silences @ sidewalk sale, prices slashed
Not sold in vending machines — they're too LOUD
They vent via Vipassana, scream to whisper
blistered escalators conspire with elevators
The gaslighting of public transpo thru loopy cameo

SARAH CAULFIELD
Akishima-shi

Dusk-light, sweat-drenched,
We meet at the station:
There are a hundred trains between ours
And the last one home, but we're still tired.
In the harsh overhead glare above the gate,
The sheen on my face is a mirror:
Atsui, ne? Hai, atsui.
The thread of what we say is like this:
Every third word now follows.
Atsui, yes, but also *itai,* also *nani, hontoni, sumimasen:*
a holy trinity of which words gaijin learn first.
We walk on aching feet, still dressed in the respectable neutrality
Of anonymous *eikaiwa* teachers.
But when we speak in English, people stare.

The convenience store sings to us when we enter;
Air-conditioning a wall of relief, we limp, moth-drawn,
Towards the freezers. We dip our hands in the cold,
Briefly consider staying there, here, forever: wedded to a 7-Eleven.
This is part of the routine. There are worse marriages.
My fingertips drift, languid, attentive, captivated,
over the limited-edition ice cream:
Even though I will choose the same one I chose last week,
And the week before:
I dread the week I will come and it will be gone.

The yen slips from my hand onto the tray, drop by drop,
Like I've sweated it out. The cashier thanks me for it anyway.
The door opens. It returns, it always returns,
It's another month until the end of summer is in sight:
Atsui, ne? It's gone dark outside. We walk by electric light,
The night song of the vending machines humming
under the cicadas. The air smells like the memory of sun.
It lingers. *Tell me about your children,* one of us begins.
How were they today? Small inhales of ice cream that sting.

Aishiteru isn't something you say out loud:
It's not something I even know if you can say to a place.
I am not sure if the grammar can expand around it,
Or absolve the weight in my chest, but you know
It's true, it's true, it's true —
So much I can barely breathe around it.
Itai. Itai. Itai.
I love this place so much it nearly kills me.

ANDREW GEBERT

コロナの世
猫のくしゃみも
こちビクッと

In the time of corona,
I flinch when
even the cat sneezes.

– – – –

– – – –

同じよそ者
からなる街にしても
ニューヨークは
だれもの街でもなく
だれもの街でもある

While both are cities
made up of outsiders
New York is a city
belonging to no one
and everyone.

東京は
どこまでいっても
だれにとっても
自分ではない
知らない
誰かの街だ

Tokyo is always
and for everyone
a city belonging
to someone
you don't know
who isn't you.

DAVID SEVERN & TAYLOR MIGNON

Madame Kicker

for Masahiko S.

Hoochie coochie cinnabom, g n t no lime, table splinter in palm
Indigo n khaki reggaement blows an air on a g string
Red tubby n calico super duper pinch bassist rips show
eno n byrne-ing bush of ghosts up on deck loop loop
US is waiting & Boredoms lay down in Shimokita coin locker
Down the tracks, a station's lights shine from ancient time
Down the flask & town's neon turns to drizzle curve moments
Rain's bow and arrows drozzle on while folk homego
Home slice left shag right duff gruffly among labyrinthian curbs
Achi kochi, m c escher-calators scuttle down to bedrock

April 19, 2019

TAYLOR MIGNON & JORDAN A. Y. SMITH
Denshi Renshi (電子連詩)

S/he it them us we ourselves benched the press for a thousand word pounds

The Mensch and the Benshi
Empty head deaded with
Bench-warmer nepenthe

Hachiko and Benji anthromorph pickin sanshin & banjo @ 9th inning stretch

Hamstrings tingling, ham-fisted rib-tickling
Loyal to a fault-line
With soil and plotline
Grew blue suede shoes
And a fedora for the aura

Mr. Beau Shpongle, trance trance this ellipsis dingle dangle does dance

But doesn't do ||pants||
Not so into }{clothing }{
=Raving= & =roving=
& cyber-punktuation
Himalayan monks kissing hunksss of defffflation

Thai fisherpeeps in Yoga pants do handplants {!} Sponsor Words::: Uniqlo
w/Yayoi & Yokoo on the go....go ala Tones on Tail Go! Gap ゲップ {!}
Zara: respectful, elegant cheapshit apparel....yay {!}

Underneath chic sheaths:: Zen-sheen Dots Mode = 全身脱毛 de
bald ≠ spectacle, my hairless little delectable
Retractable-fact Writing Hood
Wolf ear headphones
Sinking in fangs
Blissing _]out[_ to the dead TONES

Never baloney nay say ever salami yay sushi ma' omey ma' dude
irreveriblingblongitude exude a White Russian flush up, this humpty empty
dumpty a nitty gritty dingalong singalong semi-dirty ditty

Truly gritty
Unruly itsy-bitsiness
Tiddly-winking titties
Slipping doubloons into gold tipsiness
ENTER POLITICS ...
Okay, now EXIT POLITICS ...

In out in out, coitus interruptus, revolutate responsibly anarchate yr ass & yr
blinding 3rd "I" will be bound to see see, you statue girl, wicker boy, the other
others you & me flee yr mind @ land mine field free

Refills, recaps: Buddhist moonshine
Sex in an election year
Sex with an erection clearly
Wrecked in the electric chair:
                Redirected to greener pastures,
                It was downright awkward:
                                Offered the black handshake
                                Then Slaughtered by the imposters

CRTWORK BY

S I M O N
KALAJDJIEV

These glitch artworks are made by intentionally corrupting digital files and creating errors for aesthetic purposes. They are slices of deliberate damage. Neon excitement, sculpturesque architecture, and maximalist city clutter.

Tokyo is too vast and it seems there is always something going on under the surface, over your head, behind every wall, in every nook and cranny. Something you're not privy to. A fourth dimension that opens up only sometimes, only to some. These artworks aim to capture that feeling, that uncertainty, that slippery surreality.

The artworks in this volume have been created specifically for ToPoJo.

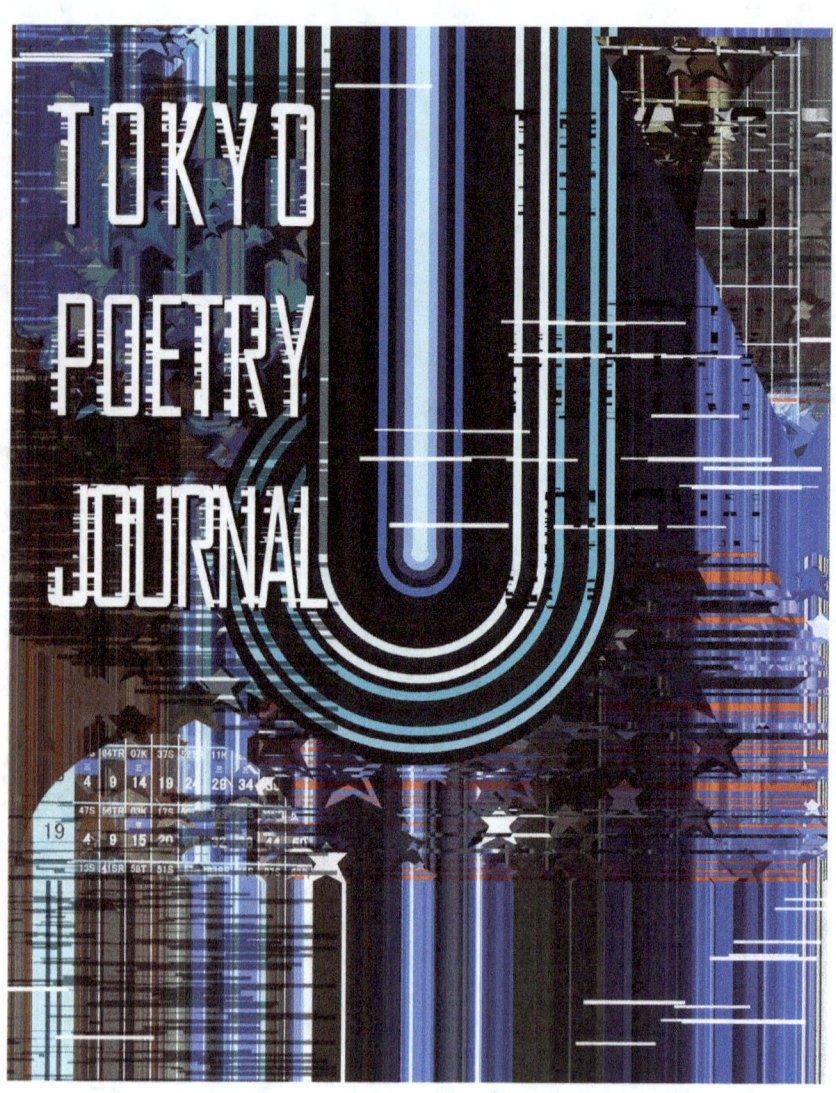

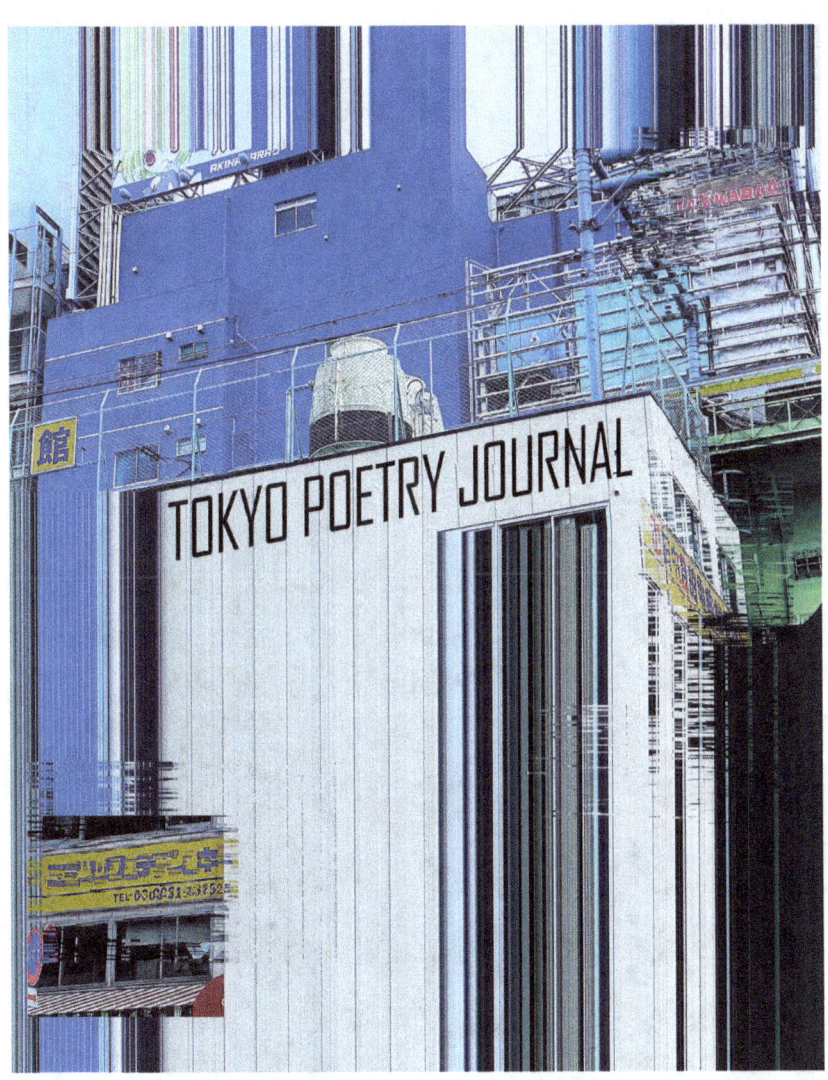

SIMON SCOTT

Night Was a Black Flower

The night was a black flower
I eat the tender petals with good cutlery and a smattering of salt and pepper
Her hair smells like fresh-cut limes in a Mexican bar
and I taste the blood in the back of my throat
The bendy feel of her reflex rubber nipples... Ping Pong
is the national sport of China
and is also popular in mental institutions, jail rec. rooms and rehab facilities
because it is hard to bash a person's skull in with a bat that small

The rest of the day looks like the sound of rivers emptying in cold mountain passes
I see fire ants crawling across cracked desert ground
Where Joan Bassett died of a gunshot wound to the back of the head on a road in El Paso,
    Texas in 1973
When the night was a red flower

The roses of rehab turned from blood-red to dark purple
We wazzed on walls fearless, our piss turning to steam in the cold sea air
Interfering with the world weather system and causing a thunderstorm above the Pacific
You wan' go boom boom Big Boy?
In the repainted hotel lobby of memory
the old push button phone is as black as a rose and an early death

We rode an unbreakable glass tuk-tuk all the way past heaven
Waving respectfully to Karl Marx, Buddha and the bass player from Rare Earth
(who were not social distancing, wearing masks or worrying that smoking causes cancer)
Stopping only briefly at the Denny's near Chigasaki Beach to wash our arses with a very, very
    powerful washlet that couldn't be turned down low
To be left with nothing but our loneliness, haemorrhoids and very reasonably priced beer
Simon says clap your hands, always make pension payments and never, never cum in a beer
    glass
During the night of the golden shower... sorry, flower

He will walk the roads of Shinjuku barefoot and no longer in love with money
To finally drink the intoxicating milk of the invisible breasts of the skyscrapers of Monday
    morning Ginza
He paid ward tax on time and, inevitably, this lead to a nasty divorce
しょうがないなあ...
His udon noodles started whispering to him in a rough Shikoku *ossan* dialect
all glutinous, starchy and over-boiled
About the night, the night, the night... they killed the flour

The night the moon opened
and all her petals
slowly
fell to earth
And from then forth
The sky was always a black black flower

ZORIA PETKOSKA K.

#ICYMI

The man who sells his skin for ad space
Is livestreaming again

This city is blooming second-degree lithium burns on us
Unpresent© like phantom pain
The clop of geta untethered pace

Sings something too similar to the jingle of the konbini

Sticky and bright

CLAIM THIS AD SPACE

Заявите права на это рекламное место.

Deadstreaming© trains

(*click here to buy rights to this word*)

Go between incomes and expenses
Like the moon they say used to cycle.
I bundle up leftover attention to use for…

SCAN QR CODE TO TRANSFER ¥100 TO CONTINUE READING

QR码以转移100  日元以继续阅读

Future Etymology Dictionary

Deadstream /dɛdstriːm/ (noun/verb)

Swipe through the cyber cemetery
Find and deadstream Legendaries

Forever at our fingertips,
Deadstreamers from the past ask no questions,
Charge no tokens.
To die, to sleep, no more.

{{*Swipe Occullus: to Neuroloan this entry*}}

_____

Neuroloan /ˈnjʊərəʊləʊn/ (verb)

Words and woes, everything is owned,
anything can be loaned.
Every neuron is a library that cannot be burned.
Only archived until your tongue is bare bones.

{{*Swipe Occullus: to Neuroloan this entry*}}

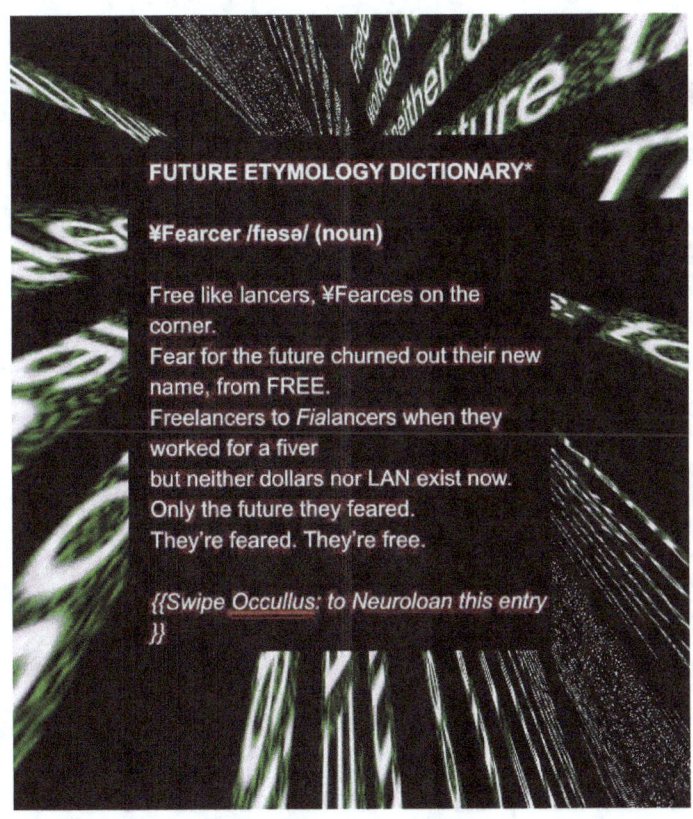

FUTURE ETYMOLOGY DICTIONARY*

¥Fearcer /fɪəsə/ (noun)

Free like lancers, ¥Fearces on the
corner.
Fear for the future churned out their new
name, from FREE.
Freelancers to *Fia*lancers when they
worked for a fiver
but neither dollars nor LAN exist now.
Only the future they feared.
They're feared. They're free.

*{{Swipe Occullus: to Neuroloan this entry
}}*

Neuroloan Replication Attempts

FUTURE ETYMOLOGY DICTIONARY*

‖Fearcer (freer/ (noun)

Free-likelancers, ‖Fearces on the
comp.
Fear for the future churned out their new
name, from FREE
Freelancers to freelancers when they
worked for a liver
but neither dollars nor LAN exist now.
Only the future they feared
They've feared. They're free.

‖(Simpa Occult is to Neureloan this epur;
)‖

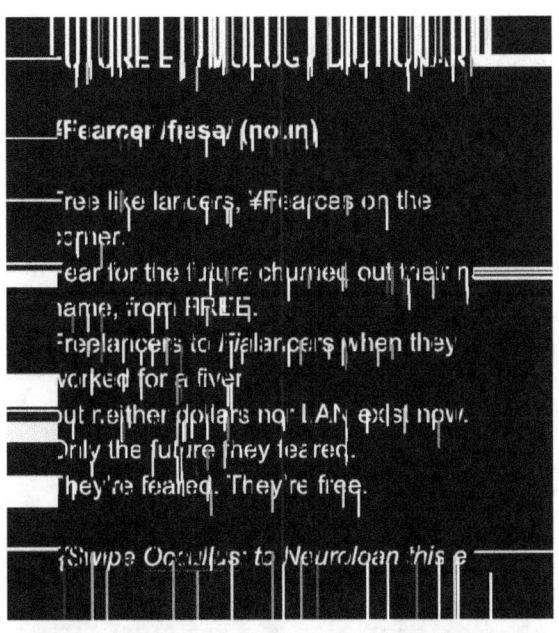

FUTURE ETYMOLOGY DICTIONARY

#Fearcer /fiəsə/ (noun)

Free like lancers, ¥Fearces on the corner.
Fear for the future churned out their n name, from ARES.
Freelancers to /fiəlancers when they worked for a fiver
but neither dollars nor LAN exist now.
Only the future they feared.
They're feared. They're free.

[Swipe Oculus: to Neuroloan this e

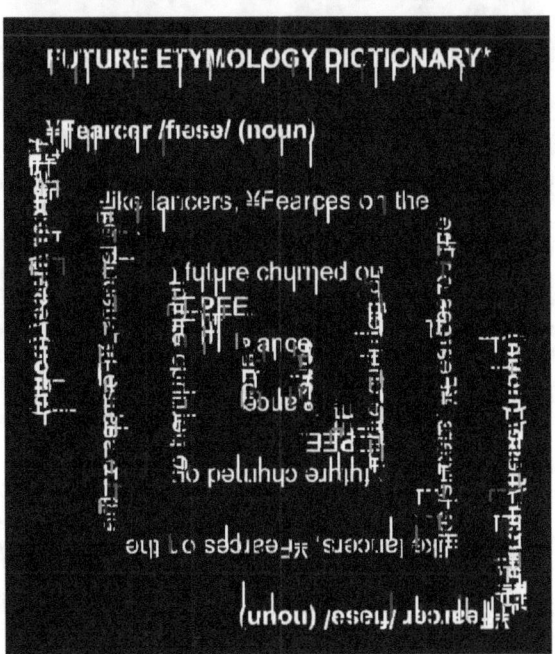

FUTURE ETYMOLOGY DICTIONARY*

¥Fearcer /fiəsə/ (noun)

like lancers, ¥Fearces on the

future churned ou
PEE.
ance
able

¥Fearcer /fiəsə/ (noun)

ANDREW HANSON

Christ Born in a Packaging Plant

Boxes that bear no gifts!
Barrack discipline! Production
fractured between huts!
Opium thrown onto the markets!
Commodity lotteries, no night skies,
banks that stilt by on the sidewalks!
Long-forgotten blockades, trailers
full of fake geese, meals sold
right out of your mouth!

Vauxhall

The cracked sidewalks teeth
the streets cariously, while nearby
the city sieges a park, and spray-cans
graffiti the day's meanings along emaciated
alleyways. By a fence, trees ooze resin,
and the outline of an insect is infinitesimally
eternalized a schematic as the cool air beats
the clouds into the cirrus wings of a strung-out
Icarus. The lamp-posts give no pause,
but by this park I have passed a makeshift memorial,
ribboned red for a known pugilist who deserves
a word which the vanishing opposition dodges
in the ring. Die of minor inconveniences
and a broad-mouthed announcer will annul
all annealed achievements of last year,
the next time a new walk is rolled out
by the neon beam of a construction worker.

Jacquerie

Wheat, fire, lines of supply,
leaves that splay into denarii—

Everything within reach
combustible, everyone
within reach retractable.

The nearby benches
barred to impede sleep.

Mirage in the fields,
where sprinklers are whipping
liquid barbed wire, & the seeds
in lines of clay bead white light.

What will crystallize into canon?

The shadow at a bus stop
the question mark, misshapen,
grappling onto the past,
that sharpens at dusk
in the hands of the laborers…

CARL WALSH

Japan Topography Suite

the earth thrusts grand
volcanic domes cloud-ward
they wear old names that cloak
like winter snow: *Annupuri, Chisenupuri,*
Iwaonupuri & Nitonupuri. Yotei hides its face in
the clouds a newer name sitting loosely on rough dacite &
andesite skin – a mountain of aliases: *Ezo Fuji, Shiribeshiyama, Makkari*
Nupuri in older, Ainu tongue, when this place was just 'a river running around the
bottom of a sheer cliff' & you & I did not sit here eating breakfast, watching the mountain's
stony face change with the weather – as Yotei erupts cloud – reminiscing on times
before names.

川

rivers don't flow in straight lines –
        they fight the constructions we place

                to constrain them; break their banks
                (because they can) gathering

raindrops; calling in tributaries –
        riding roughshod over human plans

                (we're no concern of theirs); not
                even animal in nature just latent

force, waiting for the right moment
        to rise up and swallow sand

                -bagged cities; silt crops; flood streets
                and houses in unbounded tide; alive

                in unconscious being, until every
                        -thing drains away and only cracked

                earth and string of drying puddles
                remain under the harsh light

of forgetful sun.

Like sunshine   I trip
down this valley – heels   entwined with tree
roots – hair brushed by leaves   that sweep us all
down-ward (in long calligraphic strokes).   Below, the   river
collects – sums together – will make a sea of them   yet (just add
salt). I'm foreign, a phase that will soon pass, as birds resettle in   outstretched
branches – complaining. The air here has swirled off mountains, cooled on   snowfields,
lost its way on the scree and quartz & swept by me tangling with trees & my hair   & moving
on. I pretend I'm in control but I can no more control the wind than all the thoughts that rush
through your head, on days like these…

Bento Box

九条池 Kujō ike

Reflected world ripples
in koi eyes
their tails flicking water.
In stillness
turtles pretend to be stone
drinking sun
as clouds make islands
in the sky.

地獄谷 Jigokudani

Humanity clings to the edges of this valley. Sulphuric
steam crowding air with rotten egg. I see no demons
//but they must be here – in yellowed rills
or cauldron pools or bubbling up deep
from Oyunuma pond//
in among fumarolic roll
of volcano breath, I watch you leap up steps
eager for more. Somewhere, demons watch on –
disquieted.

寺 Temple

In shimmer of upside
-down temple
I'll rake gravel before
your feet
as carp cast concentric circles –
shattering
our illusions of perfection
in the surprise death
of a dragonfly.

* * *

Moon over Kamogawa
gently crescent
backlights clouds.
As water, a living thing, wreaths
beneath Sanjo-dori, lit by
streetlamps. In the distance
a temple glows – breaking open
the night.

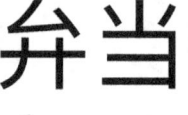

京都 Kyoto

Even in Kyoto
multistorey buildings are
interspersed between
shrines and wooden
machiya. Family Mart,

Lawson Station and 7/11 sit convenient on every
other street corner. Machines vend cans of coffee
and soft drink as I walk footpaths.
Hearing the cuckoo's cry
(if it is a cuckoo – some sort of bird anyway)
accompanied by drone of air-conditioning, rev of a
low powdered car, rattle of a bicycle.
I long for Kyoto
for all is change (and yet...)[1]

渡月橋 Togetsu-kyo bridge

On Togetsu-kyo bridge / you tear at sky
watch clouds shatter on storm mountain sending
monkeys scattering / aping tourists
into treetops.

---

[1] incorporates a haiku, in italics, by Matsuo Basho (translated by Robert Hass)

ALAN OJEDA
translated by Griselda Perrotta

I

The wind blows kind
the storm is announced
There the light reveals
some blade
A hand holding
a sword
it vibrates
and the air whispers

II
Two men wet
their katana in the river
Cherry trees exploded
on the road:
April it was
Murasama and Musamune
watched flowers run
over the water

When flowers
crashed against
Murasama's blade
they were softly cut
in halves
"That is my blade," Murasama claimed
sadly
noticing that flowers don't bleed
"Yours, Musamune, lets
flowers escape.
They touch its sharpness, and avoid it"
Musamume smiled
and in lotus
he watched the river flow

crystal clear
reflecting
the metal in his sword
reflected
in the water
"My sword does not cut
beautiful things" claimed Masamune
and took his katana
off the water
It was dry.

III
The sword comes with
the scale
the scale comes with
the matter
weighted
measured
cut
Where the useless grows,
evil grows,
for evil hides
within
decoration
Facing the sword
we measure
our usefulness
and when it rains inside
the rain calls us
and we forget
the word beauty
we do not think
and we are the rain
crashing against the stones
and against the lake
and the earth where
insects and frogs come out from
and we leave our home
to look for the home
of the world
and we are the home

we are the sword

SEIRA DUNCAN

coral

aquatic jungles
once psychedelic
musée dans l'eau
like hands a coral reaches
out to a diver
camouflaged
in the wan terrain

typhoon

carrying cacophonies of Pacific acoustics
eggs us past sliding doors
into the kitchen
hysteria reverberates in chipped lac querware
pain scrapes on 海人[1]

[1] 海人 (pronounced *uminchu* locally) a fisherman or someone with a connection to the sea. When the radical シ (pertaining to water) is removed the character turns into 毎 (every); 人毎 *hito-goto* (everyone).

KANA HOZOJI

水の塊 / Bodies of Water

By the time bodies are named bodies, they are bodies,
Like bodies of water, a collective

白人の教科書を読んで育った

描かれていたのは分断された世界で
神が創造したものには二つの世界があり
神は息をひそめていたが確かにいた
Sometimes, I still refer to that god

My hands are linked to hers; I am a part of a collective.
When story time begins,
I sit next to her 彼女の crisscross手をapplesauce style握る

マーチンルーサーキングデーの準備として絵本
を読みます
を読みます
をしている
(and later I will learn a shade of how she felt, while I give a presentation
about the bombing in
ヒロシマ, or when I am pulled over before class,
Today, we will talk, about, Pearl Harbor)

大人の私はそれを読むべきではなかったと思う
子どもだった私を守ること
は、正しいことではなくて、
可能ではなくて、
ただ、私は思う
Those stories,
read, by, bodies, pre, mature, bodies,
taught me how
to identify with the collective

知っていますが、わかりません。
を。
私が育った2000年代のシカゴの郊外では二つしか大きな水の塊は
なかった。
But this memory lacks evidence.

だってI miss Chinatown, packaged スシ, salmon rolls,
and teriyaki chicken for school lunches.
(her English name) のおうちに行ったとき、おやつに
불고기 (I apologize for my pronunciation, I would have asked,
but I could not determine, I could not find one
who spoke the language fluently so they can correct me)
がでてきて、箸は銀色で重たくて、うまくつかめなかっ
た、おいしかったこれは、foodではなく、Korean food.

I'd rather have pizza because then, I would have known, I
'd know I wasn't living in a crack in the bodies of water,
そのおおきな集合体は私まで届かない
But there were plenty out there,
見ていなかっただけ？

I cannot say that word out loud, and it is
I
who has a problem

水っぽい日本の夏は髪の毛を爆発させるし、肌を真っ黒
に焼く
I could speak for no one, not one color(s),
The watered-down collective was all I knew
, -one, , ,
A collective
I am not part of a collective,
It is I
who has
collected
it is
me
who is
a collective/塊

51

KATHLEEN HELLEN

woman as a blocking crane

a triggering

Turn. Dart. Counter-wing

The news lights up tonight like paper lanterns
They pulse and flicker, wheel into existence
                                        It isn't clear
what survives the rippling lights, gives rise to name and form
It's just another example on surveillance cameras
A man hits an Asian woman with a cinder block, holds her down, hits her
hits her on the head

He has on khakis. The kind that dads wear. A blood-red shirt that matches gashes
in her photos from the hospital
... tell me if I've got anything wrong,
if I've left anything out.... One

identified in charging documents as sister
tries to push him out the door...the sister, 66 or 67 which? *Turns....*
Counters. Tries to push him out the door
There's nowhere I can go to hold the center. I remember...

sister
Turn
Dart

The boys who sing-song-ching-chonged, threw me down a hill and broke my clavicle
They wore polyester pants, button-downs.
They draped their jackets on their arms the way a waiter
drapes the napkin for the messes at your table

... tell me if anything will be done,
if anything will come of it....

The moral arc, you know. Bending...

the house that smelled like the sea

with erasure from Executive Order 9066

the sun is shimmering in the spray, like memory in flashes like koi,
under the iridescent ripples. *You wore your soldier's uniform, remember?*

If he misses her, he doesn't say. He says what he regrets — not leaving but
the taking.
Not surrender. The old man he convinced to sell,
not his to take but still, the land taken.

*(... whom ~~he may from time to time designate, whenever he or any designated Commander~~
~~deems such action necessary or~~ desirable, ~~to prescribe military~~ areas in such places and of
such extent ~~as he or the appropriate Military Commander may determine~~, from which any
or all persons may be excluded....)*
I lock the wheelchair.

Behind the rehab cranes gather. He is floating in and out of dreams. Is it me?
Holding on to things. A photo of them holding hands. She wears a
schoolgirl's blouse,
her hair in ribbons. *Was there a pond? A clay-tiled roof like in the travel books?*

In the photo he wears a dark kimono. He is sitting in a chair, looking off into
the distance. Light filters through the gauzy curtain. On his lap a book, open.
Every now and then I check to see if he is sleeping.

The moss like silver threads floats in the cypress where the egrets roost. I
have no memory
of the house in Hamamatsu, the house where I was born. All I know of
how these things began is borrowed. Tokyo, she said, when I asked what she
would miss. Her eyes like slits I couldn't find when she was crying.
Who cares, if caring only means you suffer? If crying...

My mother posing on the beach. Behind her, fishing boats returned and
tethered to the rocks.
The tide coming in.

Every now and then I fix the blanket on his knees.
He says her house smelled like the sea.

MISUMI MIZUKI
translated by Andrew Gebert
South of the Spree River

holding my knees
i am watching the
washing machine go around
it gets dark late
so you mustn't misunderstand

when they touch stillness
people fall silent
not empty
randomly overflowing
if we choose freedom
we cannot choose
anything but freedom
there was nothing
that needed to be done

and then
the washing machine
picks up speed
still holding my knees
peacefully abiding
i become a fossil
still watching the
washing machine
peacefully abiding
i become a fossil

from *Room With No Neighbors* (TPJ Excursions, 2022)

NAGAE YŪKI
translated by Jordan A. Y. Smith

Semiotics — Spring with Cobalt

The tip of the omen
absorbed in warmth,
experience blazes hotter,
the ancient cold-air stratum peels back,
a scent half-dyed in lilac light
with its radiant behavior wets
nostalgia's parched gaze

(the rain, falling. burning and glowing,
a rain of cobalt blue.
my throat, parched. my stomach, empty. living.
the rain, falling.

Scorched from battle,
we stood on the eroded shores of
the equality we'd aimed for, turn after turn,
Spica's blue burning circumstance
luminescence, hesitance.
Whittled into regular rhythm,
heated through utterance, it shoulders transparency,
the name alone fixing a bright smile on distant future,
in a state of quiet, approaches the era
(the rain, falling. cobalt-tinted sinews of rain blaze, countless sinews radiating
light, with rich sounds come pouring down.)
Word and deed plucked by kindness
from amid equality,
I may be in the now or not at all,
spirited tones probe the cyclical monotony,
a yearly thing, blazing in the spring rain.
Passing by various founding moments,
washed away in the line-breaks of *langue*
not a whit of historical origins left unweakened,
thus no one could directly bear witness
amid welling abundance,
as the fact of existence dilutes
the certainty of death,

I mutter it's alright to be alone
being with someone can still be lonely
emotions, people too, are just information

"The rabid passion of Anglo Saxons, ultimately is a thing beyond megahertz. Actually, since the age of geography is over, even without distinctions of longitude and latitude we can still comprehend all kinds of sadness and tragedy. However, this seems to have carved the borders deeper, and the easy hearsay that comes and goes through televisions and smartphones has rendered us mere names to each other. As is the case with anyone who slothfully accepts the heaviness of being, the lights of social networking sites and electronics are incessantly rousing the deep carbon night, and my own sleep is constantly tangled in the fatigue of repeated waking and nightmares. I'm sleepy. I can't sleep. Water sounds. The color, of water. As I wake up, the weight of intensified drowsiness, on the tips of my ever more slowly blinking lashes, the flashing of electrons in the blue light, pile like snow in early spring, thus with falling asleep and exhaustion itself, nostalgic sensations fall like petals on my accepting eyelids, then the scent of the water, somehow drawn out by blue wavelengths of the electric current, gradually immersed my breath glowing cobalt blue. I was a little girl, a few drops of rain, were falling. Within the wateriness of those raindrops, as I retraced my route to school that day, I was carrying a school bag in the color of vermillion, like a cocklebur, carrying my mud-caked school shoes, and the rain turned torrents. Our apartment was at one end of the top floor of a two-story building. My mother worked nights and went to sleep in the morning, so she was usually in her room at this time, deeply fatigued maybe still dozing, and yet, I, realizing I couldn't let her see my slippers, soiled because someone had thrown them into the gutter, turned on my heels and ran recklessly, hewing a path through the falling rain, side-alley off a covered market street into the diffuse light of a cheap restaurant with a red lantern hanging from the eaves. I sat down, cradling my quaking legs and looked up to see the sky's faint glow, from which rain traced down in straight lines of cobalt-blue light. Now daytime, the red lanterns, extinguished, dejected, tawdry, sooty, even torn in places, when just then the shop door swings open, and someone came out maybe female maybe male. Either way, that rain just kept glittering, but even if I can't remember the name of the person who looked down at me, a young girl, and gave me a half-smashed caramel from their pocket, recalling my hushed ennui is enough years ago, no, years later, the winter dawn when I left girlhood behind, I watched that rain of freezing burning cobalt, dressed in my school uniform or in my job-hunting new recruit suit, mopping sweatdrops, I could do naught but watch as dusk warmed by the plasma rain quietly wrapped up summer, easing its heat. The rain is falling. Burning shining cobalt-blue rain is falling. My throat, parched. Stomach, empty. I'm alive. It's raining. It's winter now, right? No, summer. I think it was just the tip of the omen of spring. The house I lived in back then, the continual patter of rain on its sheet metal roof, the morning light nostalgically breaks through my closing eyelids fading into slumber, in the recesses of memory, the elongated scenery and signs, fading into each other like a mating pair, the rhythm seems to gradually take on the scent of Sirius. Those days come suddenly back to me, coming to greet me when I traveled back home, my mother, I recalled her lovely young voice, with its septicolored rainbow paleness. All of it, it is information. I too, from this moment on, everything. Nonetheless, someday, this and only this as yet falling rain in radiant cobalt, pouring down while raising a sound like light, as certain and singular as a dream the people have at long last managed to envision, is mine and mine alone."

< I'm alive, I'm alive   the voices
tread upon   by the sounds of a starry rainfall >

TERAYAMA SHŪJI
translated by Marc Sebastian-Jones
The Dove

On a rainy day
A gift
From an older black man

The prettiest of doves
His gift
On a rainy day.

The three of us
Then
Were inseparable

On Sundays
The three of us
Picnicked on wild strawberries.

But
One day
He stopped coming and
When I asked
"Gone to Nam"
Is all they'd say.

On a rainy day
A dove
A gift from an older black man

Far away
In the heart of the Mekong Delta
The gun he fires

In Vietnam
The dove — crippled — flies
Over the hometown of another: a stranger

Come home soon
And everything will be
As it was once

The dove
Given to me on a rainy day
Is ill.

JORDAN A. Y. SMITH

「みだれ髪神風: *Tangled Hair Savoir Faire*」

みだれ髪神風
淫らな嫌がらせ
慣れてきた矢先
阻むな
率いよ
尖端を鈍くするな
邪魔するな
チューチューしろ
たじろぐな
骨折りから指折
絶句するな
苛むな
イラつくな
な、遊ぼう
一泊二泊
♪泊まれよ、遊べ
遊べよ、泊まれ ♪
甘い
生の天下り
葉っぱ
ふとももの桃がり
パパはタカ
膝
どうぞ
ママは
虹の霞
魔法
蒸気
what does that mean
—steam—
享楽の筋肉に
包丁
先端
指す

        Baby

Kill me

Smash it

Waterfall

絶対流動性

心の　　入江

心の　　切り絵

ki ki ki ki ki ki 機会、

de de de 電車かもしれない

汽水域

時折、時が折る

年寄りの宇宙の

土に穴を掘る

吠えるパパ

もえるママ

母はハハハハ

女性に化けた

処世術

手と手と手と手を

繋いで、スマイル

君の名という

故郷に帰る

市役所「で」入る

古い池に

艶っぽい蛙

新たな旗を

水の音に捧げる

at home in the nomenclature

is it nature or nurture

we're busy *nurturing* Nature

with our Nurturing *natures*

through a culture of hatred

we cultivate naked we're rakes hey—take it

I will rake your flesh

nay—

I will rake both our fleshes

with wheat thresher

fresher than

cracked abandon

pressure

ha!

time for a refreshment

fuck it. time for a refresher—

time to see the teacher

time to eat the preacher

time to freak the speakers
time to heat the beaker
time to *cut*
the peaches
pour a glistening pitcher
of lemon water
to breathe
麒麟の
心の
ボロボロ羽衣
首筋
親しく
著しく
息苦しく
詳しく
調べられる
呪いのかけた
鎧が焼けた
欲ができた
良くできた
ぞ

And so—
I'll whisper all the things
you didn't know I knew:
I know all the drama that you
don't go through,
But act like you do.
Rose bouquet—red—
but the Violence is blue.
Every night, I buy tickets
to your fucked parade
to throw flowers round your neck
taking aim at your throat
Dope
So potent, storm can finally arrive
Can beat into my
chest
And like remind me I'm alive
(&@&@&)
Where heat converts sweat
into steam
burns: *Get it.*
But *I* already said it

We're vetted, it's copacetic
Now let it go to rest
Off your chest and let's forget it
It's bedtime. Drum time.
Vampires. Monkeys.
Thigh highs. High wires.
Balancing. Drunkly. Plunging.
Nothing goes bump
in the night, so Something
must be in the kitchen
making plump little dumplings—
Nothing says LOVE
like a roasted dove,
stuffed with oak root soaked
in smoke and blood
Nawwww—Nothing says LOVE
like a golden glove
shoved on a spike
in the bleeding stub
Inquisition—
what animal *is* this year?
It gallops like a stallion
With the heart of a bear.
My friends,
What we have here—
is some savoir faire,
What we have here—
is a world premier
What we have here—
is a braid of veins
What we have here—
will be tangled hair.
It rains.
Who cares.
I will choose love daily
Even if it nails me
音色=色気
그로케,
갑차기--왜?
quiero que el hierro que ni siquiera supiera que nos quemaremos
el horno la tierra la sierra tiembla
ya que
para nosotros
el tiempo siempre
—termina—

MATTHEW ZUCKERMAN & TAYLOR MIGNON

O Glorious Galore!

Buck rolls & bucks flow, dragon digests, splurge of words regurge
It ate cream cheese with crushed strawberries, rustic pompadour swelling and opening
Deux delishier palette pleasure round two, dragster goatee, embedded r3
Wide eyed into the eyes of time and down down down
Thust hence, Freddie King gave birth to this ditty, wit-ness
Hide away and stumble on to San Ho Zay
No way! Yazohnas is like macarolli hosanna
To all the believers on the parsnip of glory
O glorious galore of a fast Las Vegas rolling die

***

TRISH SHISHIKURA
The Bubble Economy

In the lexicon of death, you may find the following:

1. Oximeter
2. Sweat
3. Dehydration
4. Recession
5. 過労死 which, in the English language, does not exist.
6. Hopelessness
7. Asphyxia
8. Starvation
9. An enclosed gasket
10. The sound of space

Outside, there are a hundred lit lanterns mourning for the end of the Showa Period.

It was in the Showa Period that the term 過労死 was coined. In 1969, a man a year shy away from his 30s died from a mysterious heart-related problem. During an interview with the country's biggest newspaper, his parents spoke about a river. They wondered if his heart knew that it was about to strike its final pulse, wondered about his veins, if they let out a howl before they collapsed. About a decade later, the term 過労死 was coined referring to the phenomenon of the largest collective that had dropped to the ground, writhing from a heart attack. Authorities assumed this was a mass suicide by a group of twenty-somethings, but it wasn't. Death was not their first choice; they only wanted the tsunami from under their beds to bring them back to shore.

In the last year of the Showa Period, my estranged lover was born. The first person I would wake when, for the first time in my life, the Garden Town would be covered in immaculate snow. The first person I would decide I am ready to die for. He would wake in the morning to leave for work, then come home in time to bruise my palms with sadness.

When they found my father's body, they noticed his fingers were stained with mulberries which was odd because mulberries did not grow where he wept. They checked the CCTV and the last sound they could catch was the crack of his back. It seemed louder than a clap of thunder, louder than the hiss of a nation's dwindling birth rate.

An ebony curtain draped over his torso. There were lacerations on his ankles and you could tell that he had tried to sever his feet off so that he had no choice but to stay. To not go home. Perhaps he wanted to run away by rendering himself disabled.

When his ghost finally made it to my doorstep, I welcomed him unknowingly with an open mouth wider than a whale swallowing the world's largest candle. My body's first instinct was to eliminate all bodies of water that resided peacefully within my organs.

The first to leave was the lake I dug and kept in my stomach. The second was the kill that connected my bladder to my intestines. I could feel his hand brushing over my hair like a worried parent watching his child's weakness. My cheek touching the porcelain lip of a toilet. Hands unmoving. Ears ringing with regret. His vague form crouched over me, whispering: watch the whirlpool. Stare into the eye of the world.

CHRISTIAN HERNÁNDEZ

MOTOKO / 督子 / MOTOKO

Quizás en tu mirada se encuentra el secreto que he buscado durante todo el tiempo perdido/ las mañanas en que me levanté de la cama/ ciego/ el cuerpo cansado de buscar tus manos

A veces la sonrisa/ una gota de leche que hace ondas en mi tazón con cereal/ el cabello recién lavado/ aún húmedo/ y tu olor como la premonición de todos mis miedos

Caminar por la calle como un niño/ mirando las palomas en los techos/ arriba los rascacielos/ personas que cruzan la calle/ automóviles que avanzan

O quizás la tarde/ los últimos rayos de sol que se esconden en las ramas de los árboles/ un grupo de amigos después de la escuela/ camaradería/ sonrisas/ en dónde estás pequeña

たぶん、オマエの視線に俺の失われた時間をかけて探し求めた秘密がある／ベッドから起き上がった朝／ブラインド／オマエの手を探し波れ波れボディ —

ときどき、その笑顔／シリアルの入ったボウルに 波を作るミルクの一滴／まだ湿っている洗ったばかりの髪／オマエの匂いは俺の恐れている全てを予感させる

子供のように通り歩く／屋根の上のハトを眺める／その上の超高層ビル／交差点で渡る人／進み出す自動車々

あるいはその午後／太陽の最後の日差し／木の枝に隠された放課後の友達のグループ／友情／笑顔／オマエはどこにいるの

Perhaps in your glance there is the secret that I have looked through all the lost time/ the mornings when I stood from the bed/ blind/ the body tired to look for your hands

Sometimes the smile/ a drop of milk that makes waves in my bowl with cereal/ the hair just washed/ still humid/ and your scent like the premonition of all my fears

To walk on the street as a child/ watching the doves in the ceilings/ above the skyscrapers/ people who cross the street/ automobiles that advance

Perhaps the afternoon/ the last sunbeams hidden in the trees branches/ a group of friends after the school/ smiles/ camaraderie/ where are you now little girl?

Or the strange need of caressing you/ sleeping in my shoulder like a child/ the soft wind/ water sound that runs along the river/ some stars/ the moment when the night demands to keep my eyes wide open/ and beg/ because I don't want you go away

Perhaps over the clouds/ the foam mattress that takes me back home/ a bag with fulfilled promises/ a written paper with dreams/ the nights when I didn't want to sleep/ because I was afraid of awakening/ in the center of my room/ full covered with sweat/ or tears

Narita Airport, September 2002.

またはオマエを愛撫したいというおかしな必要性／子供のように俺の肩にもたれ掛かって寝ている／柔らかな風／川で流れている水の音／いくつかの星／夜に目を開けてくれるよう頼まれ／そして懇願する／そして懇願する／オマエに行って欲しくないから

または、雲の上に／家に連れて来て帰る淡いマットレス／充足された約束で／いっぱいの紙袋／夢のある手記／眠りたくない夜／起きるのが怖くて／俺の部屋の中で／びしょ濡れだった／汗か涙で

成田空港、9月2002年。

O la extraña necesidad de acariciarte/ durmiendo en mi hombro como una niña pequeña/ el viento suave/ el sonido del agua que corre en el río/ algunas estrellas/ cuando la noche me pide que abra los ojos/ y suplique/ porque no quiero que te vayas

O quizás sobre las nubes/ el colchón de espuma que me lleva de regreso a casa/ una bolsa de promesas cumplidas/ un papel con sueños/ las noches en las que no quise dormir/ por temor a despertar/ en medio de mi habitación/ lleno de sudor/ o lágrimas

Aeropuerto de Narita, septiembre de 2002.

REWIND / リワインド / REWIND

Friday night, *Evangelion* on TV:
to have a beer from the minibar
and watch, again,
the drama of the boy that wanted to be
but he couldn't.

In the solitude of my hotel room,
I understand perfectly
the pain of living among strangers.

"This is your home, Shinji"

A small apartment / the bathtub with hot
water / on the dinner table, instant food
/ the beer that Misato guzzles while Shinji
feels self-restrained / the perception of the
loneliness / the gap.

金曜日の夜、テレビでは『新世紀エヴ
アンゲリオン』。
ミニバーからビールを取りながら
存在したかったができなかった少年の
ドラマをもう一度見る。

ホテルの部屋の孤独の中、
見知らぬ人と住むことの苦痛を
完全に理解した。

「シンジ君、ここはあなたの家なの
よ」

小さなアパート / お湯の入ったバスタ
ブ / テーブルの上には、インスタン
トフード / ミサトさんが飲み漁るビ
ール / 威圧されたシンジ / 孤独感 / ギ
ャップ感。

Noche de viernes, *Evangelion* en la TV:
tomar del minibar una cerveza
y ver, de nuevo,
el drama del niño que quería ser
pero no pudo.

En la soledad de mi cuarto de hotel,
comprendo perfectamente
el dolor de vivir entre extraños.

"Esta es tu casa, Shinji"

Un apartamento pequeño / la tina de baño
con agua caliente / sobre la mesa, comida
instantánea / la cerveza que devora Misato
mientras Shinji se muestra cohibido /
percepción de la soledad / del *gap*.

I recall Mexico:
the afternoons in the gardens of the Mexican Japanese Association.

Gathered in a concentric circle, the otaku of Toluca and Mexico City toasted with a can of Sapporo beer and, in the end, Hector drank up the leftovers.

The merciless days that pass in front of us leave a trickle of salt between our hands.

Have we grown for good, like bamboo, or are we wild grass rooted among the stones?

Kansai Center, Osaka, June 2006.

メキシコを思い出す
日墨協会の日本庭園での午後。

同心円に集まったメキシコシティーとトルーカのオタクたちがサッポロビールの缶で乾杯し、最後に、エクトルくんが飲み残しを一気に飲み干しした。

無慈悲な日々は
俺たちの前を通り過ぎてゆく
手にひと塩の線が少し残る。
俺たちは竹の様によく成長したのだろうか、それとも
石の間に根ざす野生の草になったのだろうか。

関西国際センター、大阪、
6月2006年。

Recuerdo México:
tardes en el jardín de la Asociación México—Japonesa.

Reunidos en un círculo concéntrico, los otaku de Toluca y del D.F. brindamos con un bote de Sapporo y, al final, Héctor se tragó las babas.

Los días inmisericordes que pasan frente a nosotros nos dejan un hilito de sal entre las manos.

¿Hemos crecido para bien, como el bambú, o somos hierba silvestre enraizada entre las piedras?

Kansai Center, Osaka, junio de 2006.

BARBARA SUMMERHAWK

Narita to Me

Wild walk through the
Xenophobic maze of
Misapprehensions
Ironed out, flatlined any hope of
Remaining off the grid(dle)
Fone, forced into my dinosaur
Hands to track where I would be
Me
Alone in the neighborhood of
Impatience;
How do you dial up some fun, hon?
Text try:
No I don't have any symptoms you motherfuckers.
Masked, all, waiting for results
Two besties scrape me off the exit door of the airport and
Drive me mad(ly) to bed
This city, Kiyose,
Shut up, closed down,
musing on malaise...
Old crumbs on the floor
Feeding the Kafka cockroach
Crawling across my kitchen, but mine
Refugee from American macho misogyny
I just wanna be free
In Kiyose shi
I wanna be free
Free,
Me

IBARAGI NORIKO
Translated by Peter Robinson & Andrew Houwen
Station

Morning after morning
going through Shibuya Station,
taking the bus to a rural suburb —
Kitasato Institute Hospital,
that was your place of work.
For almost six thousand five hundred days
twice a day
almost thirteen thousand times
you kept on treading the walkways of Shibuya
being trodden
being trodden
by so many people
up so many steps and along so many walkways
ever so slightly ground down by it all —
still here
the traces of your footsteps,
while feeling
while missing
those traces that the eye can't see
going through this station.

Like mist passing
between mountain peaks,
springing like sighs
from somewhere in my ribs
come cloud-wreaths of sorrow.

from *Saigetsu* ("The Years"), 2007

Book Town

for Tokuo Date

Meiji-era students striding,
their slightly dirty *geta* sounding, sporting *hakama.*
Taishō students,
wanting to be *mobo*, chasing after girls.
Streets down which their kids and grandkids,
without interruption, still strut now.
At Ochanomizu Station, when I get off,
their nostalgia, distantly scattering,
seeps heavily onto the pavement and the flower
shopfronts.
Slightly drunk on its thickness,
the just-printed, freshly published books,
with a sharpness that could cut your hand, they're arranged in terraced rows,
streets filled with the publishing world's high blood-pressure.

Past the bookshop at the top of the hill
where, as a student, I bought *The Japanese Slave Economy: A History*
around the back of Sanseidō
I would always search out a small press called Eureka.
A restaurant amusingly called
Kitchen Calorie
with a faded menu stuck to the wall —
cheap curry rice prices and suchlike fluttered forlornly in the wind.
"I'm getting tired, you know, of putting out poetry magazines,"
Tokuo Date would say, with a dark voice,
when he was being serious.
Eureka — meaning "got it" — had been running a long, long time.
A two-storey wooden shop like old cloth
in a corner of an alley like in the Kasbah:
so many fresh poetry books came out here, spreading their spilled-fruit
fragrance.
A fancy muffler wrapped round his neck,
going up and down a steep thirteen-step ladder,
cynical, long-haired, skinny Mr. Date!

To what place have you gone now?

What temperature is the wind now blowing through your hair?
Though pinched slightly at the front
still your black beret remains,
that flickering, single, rich mind underneath it gone.
When I walk around Book Town
I'm sure I'll see
suddenly your heavy shadow, say, at a street corner,
or a café still dark in the daytime, a corner of Ladrio.
Our death is just a disappearance!
But the heart that thinks of the world beyond,
the death of those we miss,
with a childishness hardly different from barefoot prehistoric women
who knead earthenware pots, floats up and drifts away.

A June night.
That girl who couldn't come back in the end
to her own study room, the book left open,
has the girl in the cream-colored sweater come to meet you?
In your world,
do you have any need for a copy of *The King's Ears?*
You who also have the name of "confessor,"
with so many people's complaints, their secrets, each conversation,
how can you pack every one of them
into that sealed box?
Wherever you're trying to phone from, your voice cannot be heard.
Gloomy,
gentle,
elusive voices.
People who were kind therefore
just flick on their lighters
and gather lonely faces together.
About a single man's charm,
about where he's going,
about an irresolvable mystery,
a poet, like the eight-headed snake drinking saké, called,
"No matter the amount of capital you inject,
a journalist like Mr. Tokuo Date,
you'll never have again, definitively, never!"
We laughed, didn't we? Now
please, go ahead and tell me
more days will pass, thousands more days will pass
in your soothing voice,
like when you'd ask if the manuscript's ready.

Is it done?
Well, thanks.
Ah-ha. An elegy?
Oh great.
I'll take it.

from *Chinkonka* ("Requiems"), 1965

Word Chemistry

Rendering "philosophy"
as *tetsugaku*
was the Meiji era's terrible translation.
Rendering "chemistry"
as *kagaku*
was the Meiji era's brilliant one.
My major was chemistry
but how each element changes form,
that, and why, I never understood —
at a loss,
a change of direction,
from the poetry *speech*-radical to *temple*[1]
would lose my way
bypassing reality.
The changing forms of words, thirty years,
it's not as if I've come that far
putting in palaver and shaking the flask,
measuring the weight, mistaking
what catalyst is best used to make speech-parts react and dance?
Mind absorbed for thirty years
and yet
still not able to show
a single equation for poetry...

from *Sunshi* ("With Thanks"), 1982

---

[1] The Chinese character used in Japanese for 'poetry', 詩, consists of the radical 言 ('speech') and, on the right, 寺 ('temple').

APOLO CACHO

Apolo Cacho spent a season in Tokyo in the winter of 2018 in which he drew inspiration from the city's vastness. Working with acclaimed manga artists such as Shiriagari Kotobuki, he weaves the manga style into his detailed artworks. His strokes are very dynamic, filling the entire page with excitement, giving you an impression that the density and intensity are going on even outside the frame.

"The Abyss of Identity"

"The Past Ages"

"Adversity"

BARBARA SUMMERHAWK
REVIEWS

Miho Nonaka, The Museum of Small Bones. *Ashland, Ohio: Ashland Poetry Press. 2020.*

If the title refers to relics that can be found digging through the ruins of our boundaries, it may be that the small-boned poet Miho Nonaka can be our guide through landscapes across the globe as she flirts with silkworms and plays coy with cowboys. Through her words, we see not an X-ray of her inner being, but rather a snow angel outlining the figure of a woman in search of what it means to have a soul that wanders and wonders between cultures and languages. A prosy poetry full of imagery and metaphor that makes us feel at times voyeuristic; we're never quite sure as readers whether her smile is a smirk or a sigh.

In "Production of Silk" we find a series of prose poems that introduce us to the fascinating world of the silkworm, a creature that works hard to cocoon some value out of crushed mulberry leaves that once upon a time *"produced silk stockings for American ladies"*. Every vignette gives us sips of contrasts and droll commentary:

"The motif of a silk cocoon as the inaccessible, lyrical interior goes back to the dawn of Japanese poetics. The cocoon encases the image of the beloved, the poet's longing that keeps building inside, and in my poem it holds the mother as a mythical seamstress blue in each wrist of her unborn daughter."

Yet it is the male silkworm that spins the glossiest silk, *"finer, sturdier, whiter"*, which spells doom for the female worm who *"eats more, sleeps more, takes up more space"*.

Say what? There's the slight hint of ironic role reversal here, with the male the more elegant spinner of fine silk thread, while the slothful female eats, sleeps, takes up space; or am I over-thinking a simple image?

Wrap yourself in that silky smooth passage before going on to the sub-passage "Cowboys 2", in which two white American male poets come to visit and read *"in the heart of the city where Kafka was born"* (Prague) and where Nonaka resided at the time as a student. The Cowboys also led a writing workshop in which one of them commented that Nonaka's silkworm poems were not poetry. "I don't believe this," he said of her cocooned mother imagery. When asked later by a Filipina-American poet if there were any female poets they would recommend reading, "Ahh, Emily Dickinson?" Cowboy Y twisted his nose as if he were about to sneeze... Then Cowboy X said, "Wait, what was the name of that woman I chose for a poetry prize last year?" He asked the audience in genuine confusion.

These prose sections may not be poetry, but they resonate in my poetically gendered bones. Nonaka experienced firsthand WMPCS (white male poetic criticism syndrome) upfront and personal, in Prague where my white male poet son lives with his family. And who took me to the Cafe Slavia, the location for Nonaka's "Absinthe" where she loses herself in the imagery of a painting on the wall of that cafe, Pijak absentu (The Absinthe Drinker), of a "*man who (stares) into a woman, the Absinthe Fairy, whose body was made completely of green mist*".

Nonaka sits by the cafe window wondering about "*the inconsequence of my being there*", the poet who wanders from Kraków to Prague, to America, and back to Hachioji City and Shinto shrines, always her true self just out of sight. As women in writing workshops or rooming with women who attract us in strange ways, or pondering the silkworm's journey in creating silk kimonos we'll never wear, the smallest details we focus on could give us a hint of who we are.

In another poem in which her friend Hitomi urges her to return to Japan, not just visit, as she was doing when she and Hitomi visited the Museum of Small Bones in Tokyo, she asked herself:

"God must know why our lives are
So illogical. I dream of a power
To make small, imperceptible things
Perceptible, like the pattern of bones of a bat
In flight. The power to stave off our despair."

Could the bones of a bat do that? Or a jellyfish? A "*tree standing drenched in the rain / A border between here and elsewhere...*"? Later, in the poem "Border", she writes the tree was "*full of birds all beaks and feathers... a tree dripping with piercing cries, all mouths beating leaves. The birds and branches are one, entwined for necessary heat. It's you waiting to be translated.*"

Indeed. Isn't translation an act of liberating our collective imaginations, of freeing our words to wander where they will as we search for our own souls?

ALTON MELVAR M. DAPANAS
REVIEWS

Shuntarō Tanikawa, The Art of Being Alone, Poems 1952–2009. Translated from the Japanese and with an introduction by Takako U. Lento. Ithaca, NY: Cornell University Press & Cornell East Asia Series. 2011.

The second time I came across Shuntarō Tanikawa was through his *sanbunshi*, or prose poem, "Scissors" (trans. William I. Elliot and Kazuo Kawamura) in *The Penguin Book of the Prose Poem: From Baudelaire to Anne Carson* (ed. Jeremy Noel-Tod, 2018). In this *sanbunshi*, he, son of a philosopher and a modernist, asked, "Habit alone keeps me from using the other names. Or is it out of self-defense?" And what could be more epistemological than that? But in the aftermath of the 2011 Tōhoku earthquake and tsunami, for the first time, I read Tanikawa's "Rōsoku ga tomosareta" [The Candles were Lit] as shared by a Tumblr I followed back in the day, as well as his much anthologized "Words" where he wrote, "Words put forth buds / From the earth beneath the rubble".

Fast forward a decade to the midst of a pandemic. As a beginning translator, I found myself reading Tanikawa again, through his profiles and poems that were translated into several languages in my dream journals such as *World Literature Today, Words Without Borders, Modern Poetry in Translation, Asymptote*, and *Poetry International*, among others. The first question I asked was: How can one person possess the unlikely dual identity of being "Japan's best-known living poet", in the words of Jeffrey Angles, and one of the most inventive at the same time? Add the word 'prolific'—sixty plus collections of poetry alone, in an ongoing career that spans seven decades—and we have a recipe for envy of every poet and translator. I do not include his work translating *Peanuts* comics and nursery rhymes, and writing children's books and movie scripts; or that he also composes lyrics of songs, contributes satire for newspapers, comedies for the theater, and has had excursions into other audio-visual arts.

This current collection *Tanikawa Shuntarō: The Art of Being Alone, Poems 1952–2009*, or more aptly a single-author anthology as it could be read as one, is translated by Takako U. Lento, who also provides a critical introduction to the poems, with the addition of occasional translations by W.S. Merwin, products of collaboration with the author himself. Lento, Iowa Workshop-schooled, is a skillful translator: rendering Tanikawa's distinct poetic voice and reinforcing it for the Anglo-American reader. Her introduction is carefully crafted: in it Lento suggestively gestures how many external factors shaped Tanikawa's poetry. A good resource not only for scholars and avid readers of the poet's oeuvre, but also, on a larger scale, 20th century East Asian literature, as well as Japanologists, but also for non-academic Japanophiles and a generalist readership. Lento's introduction is fitting because Tanikawa himself attracts an audience within and outside Japan whose literary tastes vary. I find it a good companion to another anthology I have read, *Shuntarō Tanikawa: New Selected Poems* (Manchester, UK: Carcanet Press, 2015), by his long-time translators William I. Elliott and Kazuo Kawamura, who curated works from *62 Sonnets* (1953) until *Kokoro* (2015) for the above mentioned book. In the introduction, Lento discloses what translators are mostly anxious about: the perpetual tensions between literal translations or 'word-for-word' ("bringing ... the original cadence, diction, and feeling ... to be as faithful as possible to the original") and creative translations or 'sense-for-sense' ("feel [the poem's] emotional charge, and ... understand its connotations and significance"). Lento goes on to suggest that readers compare her translation and the book to those of others—Elliot and Kawamura come to my mind.

In *The Art of Being Alone*, somehow historiographical, Lento traces the expanse of Tanikawa's body of work like an aesthetico-historical timeline. After all, a project this expansive is much needed for Japan's "first poet of the post-war period" (Bownas & Thwaite, 2009). Five of Tanikawa's poetry collections have been translated here in full along with selections from other collections. This book begins with poems that are meditations on ecology from Tanikawa's first collections—*Alone in Two Billion Light Years* (1952) and *62 Sonnets* (1953). In "A Walk On A Cloudy Day", he wrote, "<Nah, I won't despair / I just miss the blue sky>", while in the sonnet "19: Vastness", he mused:

> In the vast expanse nobody notices
> Time dies
>
> I will stay aware of a vastness people can't even imagine
> I will be mindful of my life and death
> among the things that are indifferent to me
>
> I walk on   as if I were one of those
> I stop looking
> Suddenly then I begin to live

One notices here the sense of witnessing found in many forms of literature, particularly in lyric poetry. But what makes this different is the I-persona's outsider gaze, seeing things that other people don't, seeing things from a particular vantage point of the outside looking in, seeing things as a human looking out into the natural world he is both part and not part of. This reminds me of what Eve Zimmerman wrote about Tanikawa: he "meditates on life from a detached, even bemused perspective" (2007). In "A Morning Takes Shape" from *The Day Small Birds Vanish from the Sky* (1974), moreover, we find a poetic persona directly telling us:

> The morning was there

Cold water rushed out of the faucet
The smell of *miso* soup filled the room
…
I saw the morning take shape
surer than happiness, brighter than hope

As one of the founders of *Kai* [Oar] in 1953, a group of lyric poets, along with Hiroshi Yoshino, Noriko Ibaragi, Kōichi Iijima, Hiroshi Kawasaki, Makoto Ōoka, and Toshio Nakae, Tanikawa's early poems are described by Bownas and Thwaite (2009) as "fresh lyricism express[ing] Japan's new hope, an alternative to the nihilism of the immediate post-war years". In *Letteratura Giapponese* (2019), Tanikawa's poetry is also introduced to an Italian readership as a "work of polyphony in texts intended for the radio or for the visual" [translation mine]. This is not surprising given Tanikawa's interdisciplinary background in the arts. In the seemingly disparate poetic sequence found in *Fragments of a Forged Talamaikan Manuscript* (1978) and "Perspective" from *The Map of Days* (1982)—the collections which, in my opinion, established him as an avant-garde poet—that sonic and extra-textual quality is very evident.

As a reader (and sometimes, writer) of a contentious genre and form, the prose poem, I would like to mention that translations of Tanikawa's *sanbunshi*—from *sanbun*, 'prose broadly conceived', and the Chinese loanword *shi*, 'poetry broadly conceived'—are a complete turnaround, the final tying of a knot to a thread. I say this because historically, the first *sanbunshi* were translations—indirectly from English to Japanese rather than directly from the Russian original, or *jūyaku*, translations of translations—of the prose poems by Russian writer Ivan Turgenev. This made literary historians and scholars conclude that the *sanbunshi* is "conceived in criticism, then born through translation" (Mehl, 2021). Tanikawa's early *sanbunshi* had Franco-Russian influences [see "A Chair" from *On Love* (1955) and the excerpts from *Definitions* (1975)], while the latter ones showed he had found his own poetic ground [see "Postscript" from *minimal* (2002) and the excerpts from *Coca Cola Lesson* (1980)], as if his oeuvre is a representative testament to the flourishing of the genre within Japanese literary tradition. And in so many ways, it is.

Overall, this remarkable book, which comprises Tanikawa's body of works, zooms straight into the often ignored nuances of being alone, something celebrated in introspective and individualistic Japan but frowned upon in the rest of the world, but not necessarily an unhealthy, self-destructive isolationism. It also delves into the connections, external and internal, that we forge, and maybe, just maybe, how we look out into the world. In several interviews, Tanikawa would point to having a 'sheltered' childhood with a middle–class upbringing as his 'shield' from the very history that was happening outside the walls of their well-to-do household. That surely was an influence, coupled with having a philosopher for a father and a musician for a mother. Perhaps that's a germ for another book-length work by another literary scholar. Nevertheless, I may not be the acting spokesperson for all introverts, but consider this book about—and definitely a great poet's personal take and artistic contribution on—being alone getting an introvert's stamp of approval.

COLLECT THE INVISIBLE POEM

To find the location of the stamp, go totopojo.com for clues.

BIOS

Apolo Cacho is an artist born in Mexico City. He is the author of *El Taco Psicotrópico*, a graphic novel compiling tales inspired by Mexico City's disenchantment and scarcity. He has held an exhibition at Tokyo's bookstore Taco Ché, where he published a fanzine that compiled posters and enhanced graphics for punk concerts in Mexico.

Sarah Caulfield is the author of *Spine* (2017) and *Discomfort* (2021), published by Headmistress Press. She has been previously published by Lethe Books, *Voicemail Poems*, Indolentbar Press, and *Lavender Review*, among others. A twice-finalist of the Charlotte Mew Prize, two-time winner of the John Treherne Prize, and graduate of Downing College, University of Cambridge.

Mat Chiappe works as a researcher and professor of the Global Japanese Literary and Cultural Studies program at Waseda University, where he completed a Ph.D. on the relationship between Japanese and Latin American literatures. He also did a Master's on Japanese Studies at El Colegio de México. He has translated Oriza Hirata, Kohtaro Orie, Sakaguchi Ango, and Yoshihara Sachiko into both English and Spanish, as well as Hagiwara Sakutarō's *Aoneko* for the first time into Spanish (Gato azul, Noctámbula 2020).

Alton Melvar M. Dapanas (them/they) is author of *Towards a Theory on City Boys: Prose Poems* (Newcomer Press, 2021), assistant nonfiction editor of *Panorama: The Journal of Place & Travel, Atlas & Alice Literary Magazine*, and editorial reader for *Creative Nonfiction* magazine. Part of *The Sun Isn't Out Long Enough: Queer Experiences Across Borders* (Anamot Press), *Now I Know, Daylight: Responses to Untitled No 1* (1981) by Agnes Martin (Pilot Press), *Away With Words: Selected Verse — Volume Four* (Tooth Grinder Press), and others. Born and raised in Metro Cagayan de Oro in the southern Philippines, they are currently living off-the-grid and working on a chapbook of lyric essays and autotheory on the queer body.

Seira Duncan is an indigenous Eurasian doctoral researcher in the Social and Cultural Encounters program at the University of Eastern Finland.

Andrew Gebert is a Tokyo-based translator, researcher, and gentleman farmer.

Andrew Rader Hanson lives in Naples, Florida. His work has been accepted by *Clackamas Literary Review, Ginosko Literary Journal, Voices de La Luna*, and more. He was also selected as a finalist for the Key West Literary Seminar's Scotti Merril Poetry Award.

Kathleen Hellen's latest poetry collection is *The Only Country Was the Color of My Skin*. Her credits include two chapbooks, *The Girl Who Loved Mothra* and *Pentimento*, and the prize-winning collection *Umberto's Night*. Her work has appeared in *Ascent, New Letters, North American Review*, and *Prairie Schooner*, among others. Her collection *meet me at the bottom* will be released in fall 2022.

Christian Hernandez majored in Latin American literature and has a Master of Psychology from the Autonomous University of the State of Mexico, and is a former scholarship holder from the Japan Foundation and the Japan Student Services Organization. His published works include *Moratoria* (2015), *Amor Koi Love* (2018), *Essay on pedophilia* (2019), *Eternal games of love* (2019), and *Pain in the Haze* (2020–2021).

Andrew Houwen is a translator of Dutch and Japanese poetry. His translation with Chikako Nihei of the prize-winning post-war Japanese poet *Tarō Naka's Music: Selected Poems* was released by Isobar Press in 2018, with poems appearing in *Tokyo Poetry Journal, Modern Poetry in Translation, Shearsman, Cha, Tears in the Fence*, and *Poetry Salzburg*. His translations with Nihei of tanka by Kunio Tsukamoto also appeared in *Modern Poetry in Translation*.

Kana Hozoji is a poet and a student studying Japanese contemporary literature and children's literature at Waseda University. She writes in both Japanese and English, and her poems have appeared in *Incollepoetry*, edited by Hiromi Ito and Takako Arai, and *Sink Review*, edited by Steven Karl. She lives in Tokyo, Japan.

Ibaragi Noriko was born in Aichi prefecture and moved to Tokyo soon after the war, where she lived for the rest of her life. She was the co-editor of the Tokyo-based magazine *Kai* ("Oars"), whose members included Shuntarō Tanikawa and Makoto Ōoka. Her final collection, *Saigetsu* ("The Years"), was issued in 2007, the year after she died, and consists of poems addressed to her husband. Following her death, her collections *Jibun no kanjusai kurai* ("Your Own Sensitivity At Least") and *Yorikakarazu* ("Independence") sold hundreds of thousands of copies.

Simon Kalajdjiev is a Tokyo-based artist and futurist working mainly in the field of architectural illustration and future city design, as well as comics and pop culture. Notable exhibitions: "Citygraphy" (2015), "Cappadocia Reflections" (2016), "Drawn to Architecture" group exhibition (2018), and "Araknight Gothica" (2020).

Taylor Mignon is a poet, editor, translator, and university lecturer. He teaches a Kenneth Rexroth seminar at Rikkyo University and Creative Writing at Keio and Musashi universities. His poetry was described in *The Japan Times* as "steeped in the avant-garde, yet surprisingly palatable." He coedited *Poesie Yaponesia: A Bilingual Anthology* (Printed Matter Press, 2000), and co-edited and co-translated *Distant Frogs: Selected Senryu* by Gengorō (The Hokuseido Press, 2007). He led the translation and editing of *Bearded Cones & Pleasure Blades: The Collected Poems of Torii Shōzō* (highmoonoon, 2013). His newest book as editor is *VOU: Visual Poetry Tokio* (1958–1978), published in 2022 (Isobar Press). His translations are included in the upcoming anthology of Japanese experimental poetry of the 20th century (New Directions, 2022).

Misumi Mizuki (三角みづ紀) was born in Kagoshima in 1981, and now lives in Sapporo. She received the Modern Poetry Journal Prize while still in college, and her later prizes include the Nakahara Chūya Award for *Overkill*, her first book of poetry, the Southern Japan Literature Award, the Rekitei New Voice Award for her second collection *Kanashiyaru* (Beloved), and the Hagiwara Sakutarō Award for her fifth book, *Rooms With No Neighbors* (Rinjin no inai heya). *Cakes You Can Find Anywhere*, her eighth and latest book of poetry, came out in August 2020.

Nagae Yūki (永方佑樹) writes and performs steric poetry, often through multimedia, multilingual digital experiments. Her most recent volume, *Absentee Cities* (Fuzai toshi, 2019), received the Rekitei Prize. She is the co-director of the poetry-technology collective CŌEM, curating the debut project GeoPossession. Her poem "Apparatus" received the 2012 Poetry and Thought Newcomer's Award. Her collection $\sqrt{3}$ (2016) employs the language of trigonometry along with images from geology, chemistry, and machinery.

Alan Ojeda holds a BA in Literature from the University of Buenos Aires, a degree in Journalism from TEA, and is doing a Master's degree in Latin American Literary Studies at the Universidad Nacional Tres de Febrero. He is a high school teacher, journalist, and researcher, and has also coordinated the poetry and music festivals Noche Equis and miniMOOG, the poetry festival Verano en la ciudad, the Festival de poesía del riachuelo (FPR), and hosted the radio program Área MOOG. He is the editor of Código y Frontera. He published the poetry collections *Ciudad Límite* (Llantodemudo 2014), *El señor de la guerra* (Athanor 2016), *Devociones* (Zindo&Gafuri 2017), *Shinto* (Freychinelli ediciones 2020), and *Pirofanías* (Caleta Olivia 2021).

Griselda Perrotta is a lawyer, writer, translator, and professor at the University of Buenos Aires. *Frontera*, her book of short stories, was published in 2016 (Peces de Ciudad). She shares her work on her blog *Princesa de la Viruta* and on Instagram.

Zoria Petkoska K. is a polyglot, polymath, poet. She holds undergraduate and master's degrees in English Literature and Translation, with postgraduate research studies in Japanese visual poetry from TUFS. She edits and writes both travel journalism and poetry, in English, Macedonian, and sometimes Japanese.

Peter Robinson has published various books of aphorisms, fiction, and literary criticism, as well as poetry and translations (mainly from Italian) for which he has been awarded the Cheltenham Prize, the John Florio Prize, and two Poetry Book Society Recommendations. His versions of Noriko Ibaragi's poems, made with the help of Fumiko Horikawa, were published in 1992 as *When I Was at My Most Beautiful and Other Poems* (Skate Press). A substantially enlarged and revised selection from Ibaragi's work, in collaboration with Andrew Houwen, is currently nearing completion.

Simon Scott originates from Christchurch, New Zealand and is a Kamakura-based freelance journalist, writer, and poet who has been published in a very diverse range of international newspapers, magazines, and literary journals. He is currently working on a master's thesis through the University of Auckland about the Beat Generation, East Asia, and Buddhism.

Marc Sebastian-Jones studied English at the Polytechnic of North London and Japanese at Sheffield University. In addition to translating poetry and prose by Terayama Shūji and Kurahashi Yumiko, he has contributed to *Folktales and Fairy Tales: Traditions and Texts from Around the World* (2016) and guest-edited a special edition of *Marvels and Tales* on the fairy tale in Japan (2013).

David Severn is an artist and illustrator from the UK and a long-time resident of Tokyo. He studied Fine Art at the Winchester School of Art and has held several exhibitions while in Japan. He has created illustrations for books, magazines, and licensed artwork for products. His own story and picture combinations are currently in the works.

Trish Shishikura is a photographer, creative director, and poet born in Tokyo, Japan and currently based in Manila, Philippines. Her poetry has been featured in *The Mekong Review, Softblow, Quarterly Literary Review Singapore*, and the *Philippines Free Press*, and is forthcoming in *Likhaan: Journal of Contemporary Philippine Literature* and *Rogue Agent*. She was a recipient of the Ophelia Dimalanta Award in the 27th Gawad Ustetika and a fellow for poetry in the 52nd Silliman University National Writers Workshop.

Terayama Shūji (1935–1983) is best-known for his work with the experimental theater group Tenjō Sajiki (*La Marie-Vision, Nuhikun: Directions to Servants*). He was also a filmmaker (*Emperor Tomato Ketchup, Den-en ni shisu, Kusa-meikyū*), photographer, essayist, and avant-garde poet. He won a national poetry prize for his tanka at the age of eighteen, and his first collection (*Ware ni gogatsu o*) appeared when he was still in his twenties.

Jordan A. Y. Smith is co-founder of the poetry-technology collective CŌEM, producing the 3D audio hologram project GeoPossession (2022). Author of poetry and art volume *Syzygy* (Awai Books, 2020), and co-author of *Sea of Trees* and *√IC: Redux*. Co-founder of KOTOBA, the national poetry slam of Japan. Producer for BBC Radio programs on Japanese poetry and culture. Translator of many of Japan's leading poets. Curator for DIESEL Art Gallery (Shibuya). Recent past life as Associate Professor at Josai International University, and taught comparative literature, Japanese studies, and translation at UCLA, Waseda, Sophia, CSU Long Beach. Instagram @jordangiraffe

Barbara Summerhawk is ToPoJo's Editor Emeritus. In 2010, she won the Golden Crown Literary Award for best anthology for *Sparkling Rain: And Other Fiction From Japan of Women Who Love Women*. Her poetry and fiction have been published in *The Spirit that Moves Us, Poet and Critic, Printed Matter*, and many anthologies. She holds a 7th dan in aikido and teaches at her dojo in Nishi Tokyo. She always looks forward to getting through the middle of next Tuesday...

Carl Walsh lives and writes in Melbourne, Australia, on Wurundjeri land. His poetry has been published in various journals including *Rabbit, Australian Poetry Journal,* and *York Literary Review.* Poems forthcoming in *Meanjin, StylusLit, Kokako,* and *Poetry for the Planet: An Anthology of Imagined Futures* (Litoria Press). He's currently working on two short collections.

Erica Ward is an artist and illustrator from California living in Tokyo. Her detailed Japan-inspired works of watercolor and ink combine the mundane and the surreal. She often exhibits her work in Tokyo at galleries, cafes, fairs, and events.

Alvin Wong is a poet and actor from Toronto. He holds degrees in creative writing and theater studies from York University. A Best of the Net Poetry nominee, his work has appeared in journals such as *Ricepaper, Temz Review, Surfaces,* and *Half a Grapefruit Magazine.* He co-authored a chapbook with the poet and musician Stanford Cheung and photographer Scott Hunter titled *We Could Be Anything* (Crevasse Books, Tokyo 2019). He has held numerous professional editorial positions at Guernica Editions, Existere, and Inspiritus Press. Presently, he is the creative director of the multimodal arts collective and publisher Andata Express.

Matthew Zuckerman is a writer and editor who lives in Bath, UK, where he has written on blues and comedy for *The Bath Chronicle* as well as being the paper's archivist. He is now co-convenor on music for the Bath Royal Literary and Scientific Institution (BRLSI). For many years he lived in Japan, editing the small press journal *Printed Matter* and editing fiction for *Wingspan*, ANA's in-flight magazine. In 1986 he published the guidebook *Okinawa By Road,* and more recently he wrote the entries on the island group for the Japan National Tourism Organization's website. He has also edited a number of poetry collections by Paul Rossiter, Steven Forth, Fumiko Tachibana, and other Japan-based poets, as well as publishing poetry and short stories of his own. His next project is a presentation on The Art of Louis Armstrong (in person and on Zoom) for BRLSI in April.